DATE DUE

APR 07 '97

SCORPIONS

SCORPIONS

PETER MURRAY

THE CHILD'S WORLD®, INC.

Photo Credits
Robert and Linda Mitchell: front cover, 2, 6, 9, 10, 13,
15, 16, 19, 20, 23, 24, 26, 29, 30

Printed in the United States of America.

Library of Congress Cataloging-in-Publication Data
Murray, Peter, 1952 Sept. 29-
Scorpions/Peter Murray
p.   cm.
Includes index.
Summary: Describes the physical characteristics,
behavior, and life cycle of scorpions.
ISBN 1-56766-217-X (lib. bdg)
1. Scorpions--Juvenile literature.   [1. Scorpions.]
I. Title.
QL458.7.M87 1996
595.4'6--dc20   95-46108
                                 CIP
                                 AC

TABLE OF CONTENTS

When night comes, the desert is very quiet. You might hear a coyote howl. Most of the time you hear nothing at all. But under the ground, and beneath the rocks, and in the hollows of dead trees, things are moving.

A beetle pokes its head out from under a rock. A few feet away, a hairy leg comes out of a hole in the sand. Another leg comes out, and another. Pretty soon there are eight of them. They are attached to a giant, hairy spider. The spider is looking at the beetle. But there is something else looking at the spider.

A scorpion!

Scorpions live in the desert.

WHAT DOES A SCORPION LOOK LIKE?

The spider thinks it will have a beetle for dinner. The scorpion eats beetles too. But not when it can have a fat, juicy spider.

Both spiders and scorpions are part of the group of animals called **arachnids**. Arachnids have eight legs, a hard outer body, and **pedipalps**. The spider's pedipalps look like two extra legs in front. The scorpion has pedipalps that look like a lobster's claws. It uses them to grab its dinner. Tonight, it plans to grab this tasty-looking spider. The scorpion doesn't know that the spider is a relative. Even if it did, it wouldn't care!

A scorpion has pedipalps that looks like a lobster's claw.

WHAT MAKES SCORPIONS DANGEROUS?

The scorpion has trouble seeing the spider. Even though scorpions have several eyes, they don't see as well as humans. A set of comb-like organs on the scorpion's belly can feel the tiny vibrations made by the spider's movements. It raises its claws high above its head and charges! The spider rears back, waving its legs in the air, exposing its sharp **fangs**. It is bigger than the scorpion, but the scorpion has one weapon the spider lacks—its deadly tail!

Scorpions have several eyes.

HOW DO SCORPIONS CATCH THEIR PREY?

The tip of the scorpion's tail has a sharp stinger, and it's loaded with poisonous **venom**. Grabbing the spider with its powerful claws, the scorpion whips its tail forward faster than the eye can see. The stinger stabs into the spider's body, again and again. Deadly poison **paralyzes** the spider. The scorpion backs away and waits for the spider to die.

Then it sits down to supper. Scorpions are slow eaters. It might take the whole night for the scorpion to finish its meal. Then it will crawl back under a rock or log and not eat again for days.

A scorpion's tail has a stinger loaded with poisonous venom.

WHAT ELSE DO SCORPIONS EAT?

A whole spider is a big meal for a scorpion. Usually, scorpions prefer smaller meals such as beetles, moths, or worms. A scorpion doesn't go chasing after food. It hunts by sitting still and waiting for an insect to come bumbling past. When it feels the insect's vibrations, the scorpion grabs the insect with its claws and eats it. It only needs to use its stinger if the insect is especially large or strong.

If dinner does not arrive by dawn, the scorpion crawls back into its hiding place. Scorpions do not like to show themselves during the day.

A scorpion in Texas waits on a rock.

Scorpions live in warm places. They are found in the deserts of North America, and in the rainforests of South America. They are also found in Europe, Africa, and Asia.

Before the dinosaurs, more than 350 million years ago, scorpions crept through the ancient forests. They were among the first animals to crawl out of the ocean to live on land. Scientists have discovered **fossils** of scorpions sixteen inches long! Scorpions today don't get quite that big. Most of them are only a couple of inches long. But one African **species** can grow to eight inches. Imagine turning over a rock and finding something like that!

A scorpion lives in warm southern California.

HOW DANGEROUS ARE SCORPION STINGS?

The sting of a scorpion is enough to kill a spider, a beetle, or a mouse. But what would happen if you were stung?

Well, you wouldn't like it. Usually, a scorpion sting is like getting stung by a bee. But some scorpions have a powerful venom that can make a person very sick. In parts of Mexico and India, where deadly scorpions are common, thousands of people have died from scorpion stings.

The *durango scorpion* is one of the world's most deadly scorpions.

Most scorpion stings happen when scorpions wander into houses at night looking for something to eat. In the morning, when it gets light, they hide in small, dark places. Outside, they can hide in old logs or under rocks. But inside a house, where there are no rocks or logs, they might hide under bedcovers or in the toe of a shoe. People who live where there are a lot of scorpions learn to check their shoes before putting them on!

A scorpion in southern California hides on a rock.

In the United States, the only scorpion whose venom is strong enough to be dangerous is the *sculptured scorpion* and its close relatives. This small, yellowish scorpion keeps its tail curled to the side, so it can hide under the bark of dead trees. A sting from a sculptured scorpion can cause vomiting, numbness, and difficulty breathing. The sting must be quickly treated, or the victim can die. The sculptured scorpion lives only in southern Arizona.

The sculptured scorpion has dangerous venom.

HOW ARE BABY SCORPIONS BORN?

Scorpions are mostly interested in two things. They like to eat. And they like to make babies.

When a male and a female scorpion meet, they grab each other's claws and circle around and around. They touch their tails together. It looks as if they are fighting. Sometimes they do this mating dance for hours.

Finally, the male drops a small packet of sperm on the ground, then leads the female over it. The female takes it into her body, and they separate. The male scurries away. If he's not quick enough, he might get eaten! The female gets pretty hungry after all that dancing.

A male and female scorpion perform a mating dance.

The female scorpion does not lay eggs, as her relatives the spiders do. Instead, she gives birth to tiny, fully formed scorpions. The baby scorpions climb onto her back. For the next two weeks, the tiny scorpions get a free ride.

Scorpions grow by *molting*. They shed their outer layer, their body expands, and their new skin hardens into a protective layer called an *exoskeleton*. As soon as the babies molt for the first time, they leave their mother. They are on their own. Scorpions must molt seven or eight times before they are fully grown.

A durango scorpion carries its babies on its back.

DO SCORPIONS HAVE ENEMIES?

The life of a scorpion is not all stinging and eating and making baby scorpions. They also have to avoid being eaten. A number of larger animals think that there is nothing tastier than fresh scorpion. The sparrow-sized elf owl has learned to clip off the scorpion's stinger. Bats, lizards, roadrunners, and desert mice also eat scorpions. Even scorpions eat other scorpions.

Scorpions are in danger of being eaten by larger animals.

Scorpions have lived on this planet much longer than people. They are quiet, shy, and like to be left alone. When a scorpion stings a human, it is because it is defending itself. If you were taking a nap inside a shoe, and a giant smelly foot suddenly smashed you into the toe, what would you do?

Scorpion's are quiet, shy, and like to be left alone.

GLOSSARY

arachnids (ah-RACK-nidz)
Anthropods that have a body divided into two parts.
Spiders are arachnids.

exoskeleton (EECK-oo-skell-ah-ton)
An outside hard covering of an animal. As scorpions grow they
develop an exoskeleton.

fangs (FANGZ)
A long sharp tooth used to catch prey or secrete poison. A scorpion
grabs a beetle with its fangs.

fossils (FOSS-uls)
A remnant of a past plant or animal preserved in the earth's crust.
Scientists have discovered fossils of scorpions sixteen inches long.

molting (MOLT-eng)
To shed the outer layer of the body. Scorpions molt as they grow.

paralyze (PAIR-ah-lize)
Complete or partial loss of movement in the body. A scorpion uses
its venom to paralyze its prey.

pedipalps (PED-e-palps)
A second pair of claws near the mouth of an arachnid. A scorpion's
pedipalps look like lobster claws.

species (SPEE-sheez)
A class of animals having similar features. Some species of scorpions
can grow up to eight inches.

venom (VENN-um)
A poison secreted by some animals. Scorpion venom can paralyze
the scorpions prey.

INDEX

CUMBERLAND
SUNNYVALE, CA